Autumn Garden

秋の庭

Autumn Garden

Michael Boiano

Dedication

To those who've huddled a bit closer through many an autumn and have emerged, still with me, on the other side of winter. And with compassion and sadness to those whose presence and warmth could not survive winter.

And with gratitude to Job, a friend for all seasons, who rescued this little book when others faded and fell like the leaves of autumn.

Preface

An autumn garden,
like the morning following
a noisy festival.
Like my heart when she had gone,
sweet memories and deep sighs.

Pale light, muted colors, a hush over what, seemingly only moments ago, was a riotous celebration of life. Time to wistfully reflect on the fun, the abundance, the antics and discoveries, and the intoxicating sense of the fullness of life in all its boisterous, heart-pounding, joyful mayhem.

Plants in autumn have followed their cycle, their leaves curl, take on color, drop away, and they seem to collapse in on themselves, spent. The birds have gone, leaving behind abandoned nests so recently the scene of industry and new life. Spider webs hang in tatters, small egg pouches wedged into cracks in the fences awaiting Spring. The frogs drag themselves wearily, heavily toward long slumber in the earth beneath the sheltering plants.

And our hearts, still full of that festival called summer, sigh over the waning of passing loves and shorter days. Autumn is in each of us mindful of the feast of summer and the smaller world we'll inhabit behind frost-heavy windows, rattling door frames, and the hush brought by the insulating cover of snow soon to come.

Autumn loves, those passionate hugs now muffled by thick sweaters, cooler days drawing us closer in drafty cafes, sharing solace in each other's warmth in a chillier landscape that, shuttering itself, braces for the monochrome silences of winter. And autumn longing — when is missing someone ever so acute as in this season? Early evenings, longer nights, the moon seeming larger, more a presence, the tawny rice fields abandoned, and dry, windblown leaves scuttling round our feet as we head more hurriedly toward home. There's an edge of decay to those leaves whose golds and reds have darkened beneath our feet and an awareness that some neighbors, some loves, may not emerge on the other side of impending winter. Sometimes, walking alone through such evenings, we surprise ourselves by uttering aloud the name of a loved one who, tonight, is too far from our embrace.

Autumn is a powerful season that seems to hover at the edges of other seasons. It is more than a season, more a state of mind. Winter is a state of suspended animation and silence, but autumn with its flavors, and colors, and exhilarations, its energy and its lengthening shadows, is what takes us there, a signpost drawing us on or fading for a time behind us, never wholly out of mind and then, suddenly, before us again each year. The autumn garden, in its own way, with its untenanted spider webs and cicada shells, and its dried leaves with their memories of a thousand shades of green, is as abundant in its own way as the gardens of spring with their small but heart-lifting miracles, and summer with its sumptuous, lusty depth of life which says dance, drink, laugh and love while you can, for autumn's chill and sun splashed leaves of gold lie just on the other side of tomorrow, in the season that most inspires the Japanese sense of "mono no aware" — a deep, gentle sadness about the impermanence of life:

We are but shadows
moving lightly, fleetingly
over the surface.
Noticed by some, barely seen,
they look again and we're gone.

Michael Boiano, Bangkok, Thailand.

"…your dream has autumn eyes."

A.R.

"I notice Autumn is more the season of the soul than of nature."

Friedrich Nietzsche

*"This is the light of autumn, not the light of spring.
The light of autumn: you will not be spared."*

Louise Glück, from "October"

*"Those who understand
know the garden is never gone,
look and you'll find it.
It's just moved into our hearts
and is there when we need it."*

Michael Boiano

Foreword

It's hard, lately, not to feel a sense that the world as we know it is winding inexorably toward some kind of ending — that a darkness is approaching the other side of which, if we do come through to, we may not recognize at all. In a way, this same sense runs through Michael Boiano's latest tanka collection, *Autumn Garden*. But it would be a mistake to call it "apocalyptic" in the western sense. Here the sense is not of impending doom, or resignation, but the quiet sense of heightened value that comes from realizing that things as they are cannot last.

The voice behind *Gaijin Diary*, Boiano's 2018 collection, was an observer — one who saw deeply into everyday human life even from the outside. But *Autumn Garden* is less concerned with what is going on now in the streets and in the cafes. The people we meet here are more often shadows of memory, or like the girl who sneezes from the other side of a dark alley, there is only a moment of brief connection with nothing ever fully revealed. Rather, from the very beginning, autumn is a drawing inward. In Part I of the collection, entitled "Longing", we feel human connection not in isolated instants, but begin to see the underlying rhythm. A love thought long lost to the past returns as bright as ever through letters found folded in a book:

> *Like flowers given,*
> *these letters between lovers.*
> *They quicken the heart*
> *and then are tucked into books,*
> *discovered anew one day.*

The photographs accompanying some of the tanka, like the poems themselves, create a moody scene, immediate in their details but elevated from the constraints of documentary or portraiture by a haze of half-remembrance: a spider's web, an unmade bed, a now-disembodied soft smile.

And if there is an impulse, familiar from *Gaijin Diary*, to depart this world like a lover, there is also a deep sense that nothing is ever really past, that like the frogs who sink to the bottom of the pond in the autumn, everything always returns. This is the theme of the second part of the collection, "Nature". With the coming of an autumn night, the speaker longs to be set free like a bonsai in the forest — but still:

As long as there are birds
and tree boughs swaying above,
I might as well stay.

Here there is no resignation, nor a morbid longing for death — even the tiredness that sometimes emerged in *Gaijin Diary* is gone — but rather a recognition of how the value and beauty of life depends on its eternal rising and passing away.

As the photographs throughout the collection illustrate, if the object stands in less sharp relief, it casts all the deeper of a shadow. In an autumn midnight, nature points towards transcendence, and as the collection moves into the third and final part, "Light and Shadows", the poems are increasingly suffused with a sense of the divine. All the beauty of life and this earth is but "the passing of shadows, light yielding to dark" — and yet, "we too are part shadow," and "from us, sometimes, comes light." It's hard not to see the collection as a progressive transcendence from the fleeting nature of human life and love, to the eternal recurrence of nature's rhythms, to the ultimately unknowable but ever-illuminating light of divinity. Each tanka in *Autumn Garden* thus embodies this shadow-play between light and dark, here and past and already beyond.

Taylor Kloha, University of Illinois, August 2020.

Each of the seasons
is felt deeply within us,
the seasons of self.
Today the autumn outside
exactly mirrors my heart.

When autumn descends,
houses close in on themselves,
people move inward.
And so do we, in our hearts,
in this quiet and closed time.

Like my memories,
the leaves drift across my path.
I notice, move on,
thinking how alike they are,
so beautiful and so dead.

Introduction: about Tanka

In Japanese literature, tanka — which translates as "short song" — describes a five-line, 31-syllable poem that has, since the 7th century, been the basic and most conservative form of Japanese lyrical poetry for over 1,300 years. Tanka have specific syllable requirements and employ various literary devices such as metaphor and simile; they don't rhyme and like haiku, are written in short lines. Unlike haiku, they do not require a "kigo," or season word. Tanka in English have, until recently, adhered to a set syllable count as follows 5-7-5-7-7. Tanka (or "waka") were the preferred poetic form of the Japanese Imperial court. Japanese nobles competed in tanka contests, and couples of that era often expressed their sentiments by exchanging tanka. The earliest anthology, the mid-8th century Man'yōshū ("Collection of Myriad Leaves"), contained nearly 5,000 poems written about love, longing, death, the beauty of the natural world, the evanescence of all life, and the concerns and preoccupations of simple day to day life.

My first encounters with tanka were with the poems of Ono no Komachi (825 – 900) and Izumi Shikubu (born 976), two notable figures in Heian era poetry. Within the framework of 31 syllables, they described longing, love, and sadness within the context of nature and the awareness of passing time, of eternity itself — sublimely beautiful and, for this writer, deeply mirroring my own romantic feelings and strong connection to the natural world and its seasons.

There were so many tanka poets who inspired me, who captured my heart, and who gave me this wonderful tool for expressing my own state of mind and heart, the longing I have felt, and the acute awareness of the evanescence of life I felt even as a young man. A few who come to mind at this writing are Ryokan Taigu (1758 – 1831) who was said to be a hermit monk, but one who profoundly enjoyed the company of others and got into rough and tumble grass-throwing "fights" with local children; Otagaki Rengetsu (1791 – 1875), a Buddhist nun who made pottery to support herself and would inscribe her exquisite poems into the wet clay before firing; and Kakinomoto no Hitomaro (662 – 710) whose poetry I carried with me on long hikes into the mountains of Tohoku, Japan, along with a volume of Basho's haiku.

I also made the happy discovery of the work of one of my very favorite poets, Ishikawa Takuboku (1886 – 1912), a major figure among the Romantic poets of the late 19th and early 20th centuries. He declared that his poems were "made with both feet upon the ground". It means poems written without putting any distance from actual life.

They are not delicacies, or dainty dishes, but food indispensable for us in our daily meal. To define poetry in this way may be to pull it down from its established position, but to me it means to make poetry, which has added nothing or detracted nothing from actual life, into something which cannot be dispensed with." His books "*Romanji Diary*" and "*Sad Toys*" were particularly exciting for me, showing that tanka could be used to describe everyday life and feelings, that beauty could be found in the simplest of circumstances.

There were contemporary tanka poets who influenced me. James Kirkup, who taught and wrote in Japan, was a prolific tanka poet widely appreciated by Japanese people; it was my good fortune that he found something appealing in my own writing and he became both a mentor and, over the years, a friend. In his last letter to me before his death he described himself a fan of my work — such was his generous nature. He was a strong proponent of maintaining the 31 syllable count even in English and this continues to shape my own work — sometimes I will let a line go too long or too short and I can imagine him gently calling me to account for that. For better or worse, that discipline has fallen out of favor in the world of English tanka poets, but I continue to write in the way that he taught me. I like the look, and rhythm, the feel of these poems, and effort required in composing them. Another contemporary poet I've enjoyed is Machi Tawara who was responsible for revitalizing tanka for modern Japanese audiences. As a result of her influence, "tanka cafes" began to spring up in Tokyo and Osaka where customers would write poems on their smartphones.

All of these writers — and so many more — have influenced and inspired my work, and I am grateful to all of them. My great wish is that my own small books might also, in turn, inspire others and become a part of the great tradition of tanka. My books are my small way of showing my gratitude to all the better writers who came before me. Happily, some of my students have tried writing them. Imagine that.

And here is where I will stop, and invite you to look through this book for yourselves. No need, really, to think much of form, or history, or syllables, but simply allow yourself to feel the poetry as I did with the work of Ono no Komachi and Takuboku Ishikawa. Perhaps there is something that resonates with you, something that you recognize, something that may make you put down the book for a few moments of reverie and reminiscence. And if what you find here may cause you to pick up a pencil and write some tanka of your own, it could be the beginning of your own journey with poetry, and how absolutely wonderful that would be!

There it is again
out the corner of my eye,
a passing angel.
There for an instant then gone,
its purpose unknown to me.

Longing

慯

A breakfast picnic
beneath a tree in the rain
in Ueno park.
By the time the sky had cleared
we had parted once again.

手探りの
我が暗き部屋に
ランプ追う
あの夏の夜の
君を求めて

In my lightless room
groping for a lamp, almost
expecting her voice,
so strong are the memories
of a few nights last summer.

It's all long ago,
and it's all just yesterday,
a constant presence:
warm cafes, pale morning light,
and the way she looked at me.

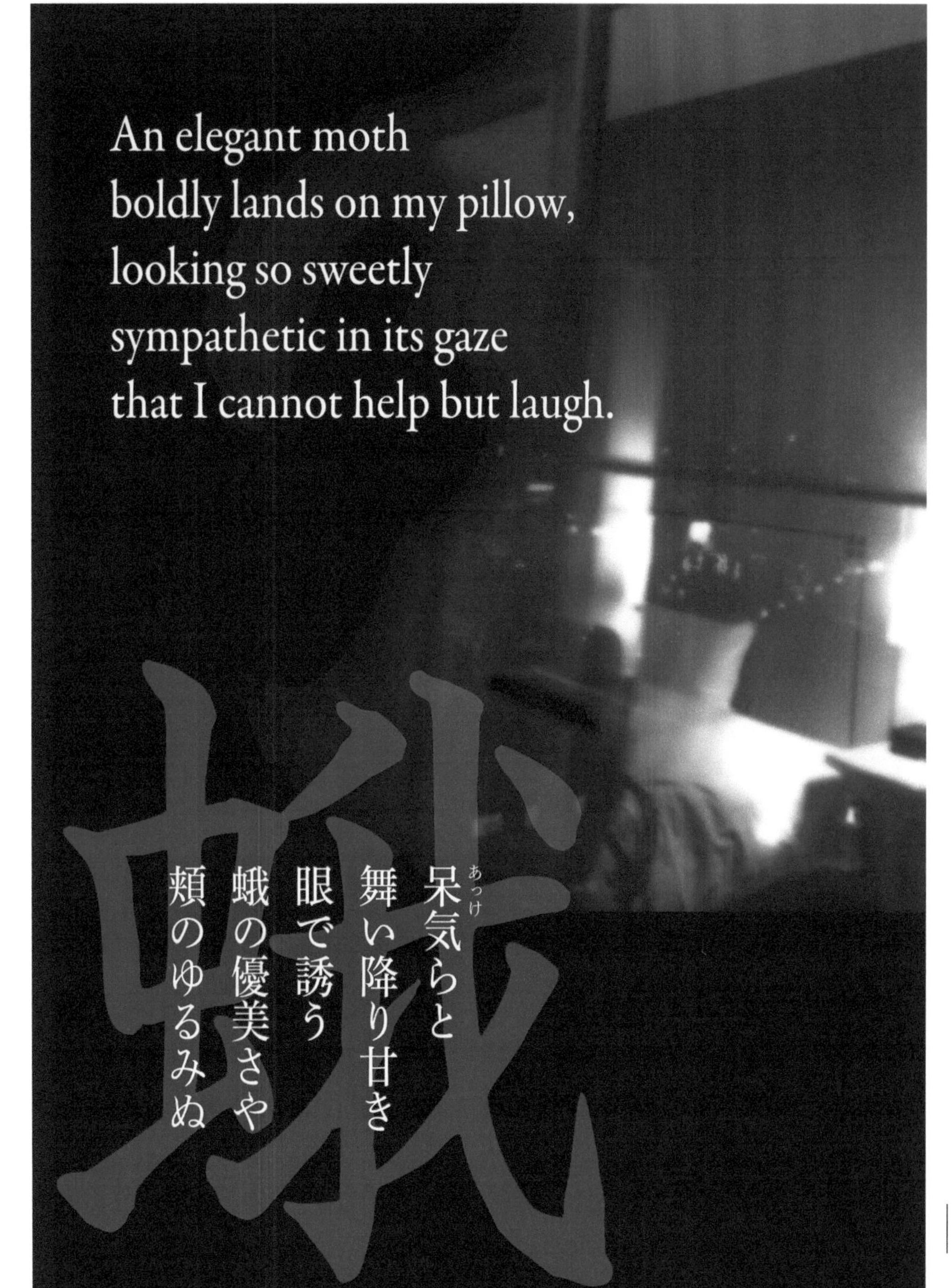

An elegant moth
boldly lands on my pillow,
looking so sweetly
sympathetic in its gaze
that I cannot help but laugh.

呆気らと
舞い降り甘き
眼で誘う
蛾の優美さや
頬のゆるみぬ

断片粒
綺羅々と寄せ来て
夢うつつ
花の顔
我が胸に落つ

Urgent, insistent,
part memory and part hope,
she came to my dreams.
So real did it seem to me
that waking, I reached for her.

From that first hello
we are preparing to leave.
Everyone we know,
they're an image that lingers
as we quickly blink our eyes.

If she had not left
me here defenseless against
these long summer nights,
how could I have understood
the sad music of crickets.

彼女失せ
蟋蟀奏でる
哀音に
気怠き夏夜
増して長らむ

I recall her hand
curled lightly within my own,
her eyes on my eyes.
Our days were like forever
and yet they passed with cruel speed.

Wish it were you here
missing me as I do you,
sending birthday poems.
I talk to you every day
and put kisses into the wind.

That café table
where she first reached for my hand
is empty today,
waiting for a new couple
more favored by fate than us.

Outside, a grey wash,
it spares me the day's details
and sends me inward.
How do the birds find their nests?
How can my heart find its home?

Standing near my door
watching the rain as it falls
into my teacup,
counting the tiny splashes,
waiting shamelessly for mail.

扉そば
隠れなお見る
雨音ティーカップ
その雫（しずく）見つ
君の文渇（ま）つ

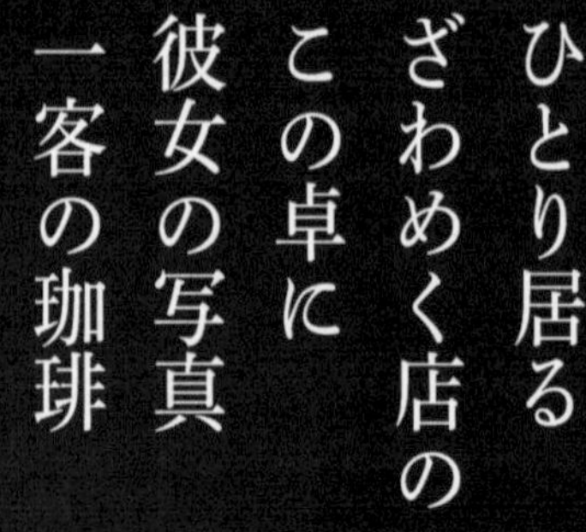

一客の珈琲
彼女の写真
この卓に
ざわめく店の
ひとり居る

My table for one
in this lonely coffee shop
crowded with couples:
one coffee, an empty chair,
her photo for company.

Of her autumns now
I can only imagine,
for she is far away,
I hope they are kind to her
and that she remembers me.

My empty garden
and this vacant letterbox,
like my patient heart:
all waiting to be filled,
yearning for one more summer.

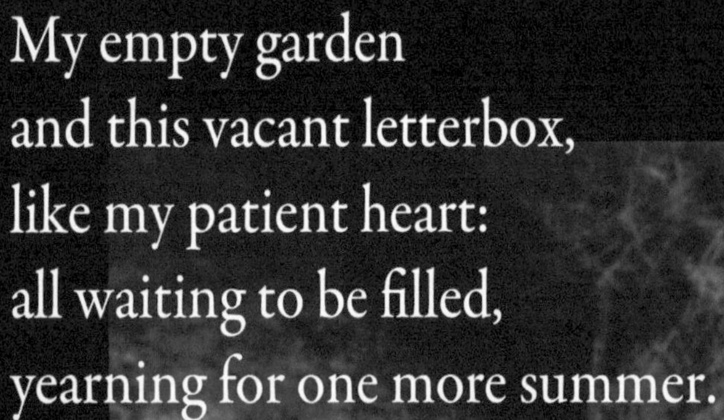

虚しさや
ポストの中身
庭景色
こを埋むらんや
もうひと夏で

I miss autumn hugs:
both of us padded in coats,
cheek to icy cheek,
the scent of leaves and wood smoke,
her cold hair against my face.

One day, embarrassed,
a woman confessed that she
had been watching us.
With sad eyes, she told us how,
she too had once been so in love.

Like flowers given,
these letters between lovers.
They quicken the heart
and are then tucked into books,
discovered anew one day.

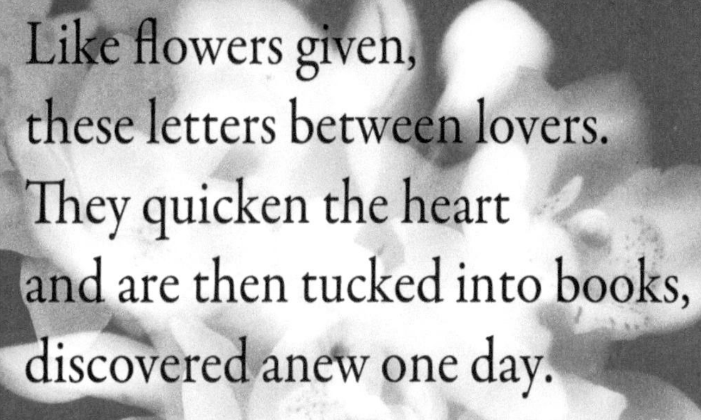

恋文は
花もらうよに
胸ふるえ
素晴らしき日々
生まるる気ぞせり

When last we parted,
as the airport bus pulled out,
we both held our gaze.
Then slowly she raised her hand
in what seemed a benediction.

A sad eloquence
in the colors of autumn,
like the last kind words
shared between parting lovers,
weary and saying goodbye.

Nature

自然

A light snow falling
in the indigo night sky,
four large crows take flight.
Why this memory today,
here in the bright summer sun?

秋の庭
主なき蜘蛛の巣
蝉の殻
枯れ葉に宿るや
緑蔭の跡

This autumn garden:
untenanted spider webs
and cicada shells;
dry leaves with their memories
of a thousand shades of green.

Set free a bonsai,
take it away to the woods,
and unbind it there.
Let the roots stretch into the soil
and let it reach to the sky.

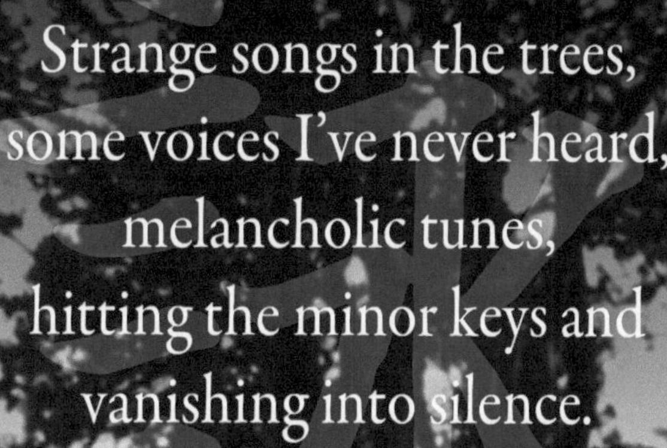

Strange songs in the trees,
some voices I've never heard,
melancholic tunes,
hitting the minor keys and
vanishing into silence.

不可思議に
木漏れて届く
幽愁歌
憂しき調べは
静寂に消ゆ

囀りの
途切れてもなお
声高く
都会の鳥や
歌 忘れじと

It begins again,
then stops short, mid-crescendo,
beyond my window...
a city bird has somehow
managed to forget its song.

Somewhere near a dog barks,
though silent, I feel the trees move,
a bird tries a few notes.
And me there, I am with them
my heart pounding in unison.

Hard to count on much
in the doings of people,
their love and their vows.
Nature seems the only truth,
its chill winds and fallen leaves.

儚きや
人の誓いし
愛誠
風と落ち葉の
天理に及ばず

Headful of worries,
I took myself to the street
under the dark trees.
The cicadas' song lifted
my spirit high into the boughs.

As long as there are birds
and tree boughs swaying above,
I might as well stay.
These joys are within my reach
and keep me tied to the world.

The light of the moon
illuminates my way home
and shines in my dreams.
Its pale light reveals the path
to the past, to other worlds.

One Sunday morning,
on the window of the cafe,
a huge butterfly.
My heart pounded as I watched it
launch itself into the day.

Strange songs in the trees,
some voices I've never heard,
melancholic tunes,
hitting the minor keys and
vanishing into silence.

Like nature itself,
we begin again and again,
in our struggle to grow.
In this way the human heart
evolves to become Divine.

The sky lowers and
colors become muted, flat.
My own heart quiets
like those frogs in my garden,
slumbering with dreams of spring.

見上げるや
空平かに
色鈍く
土中の蛙の
微睡み 想う

In the darkest night,
deep forest, brooding shadows,
I wander alone.
The starlight is no solace,
for these stars died long ago.

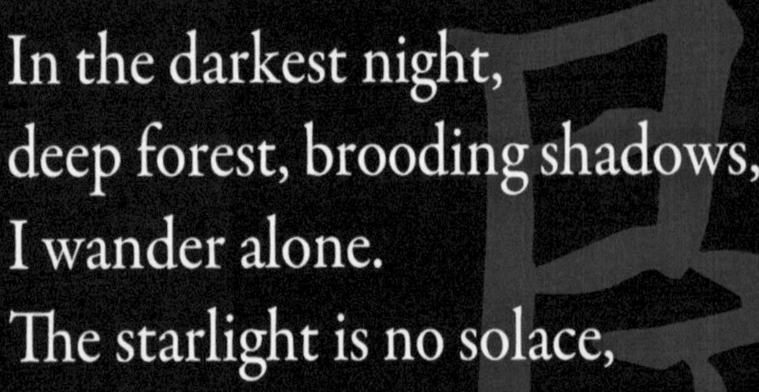

星あかり
消えし森蔭
黒々と
ひとり佇み
闇を追うらん

The scent of dry earth,
of dust disturbed on concrete
in a sudden rain.
Later, in darkening lanes,
life stirring beneath the leaves.

When I was a child,
trees were mysterious giants
possessing secrets.
I sensed spirits in their boughs,
a haven for human souls.

朝を待つ
我に瞬く
星々の
木暮の木々に
揺れつ重ぬる

Waiting for morning,
few stars in this night-bound world
witness my vigil.
Outside, beyond, dark trees sway
to their own private rhythm.

Flowers floating by,
not sakura, but close enough
to quicken my pulse.
All the sweet flowers I've seen fall,
all the dear friends gone too soon.

Two plants repotted
in the morning sun outside,
waiting for water.
I kiss a top leaf of each
before trudging off to work.

Deep within winter,
small creatures hibernating
far beneath the snow.
I wonder if they'll awaken,
and if I'll see another spring.

日の本に
居残し生きる
分霊の
彷徨い往くか
路地や深山に

A part of my heart
was left behind in Japan
and there it lives on,
a ghost that roams the alleys
and the hidden mountain shrines.

Light & Shadows

明暗

Sunlight and shadows,
gliding over tree-tops,
light shifts and moves on.
I think of my friends who've died
and how like shadows they were.

Evening shadows steal
across the chair where I sit.
I reach not for the lamp,
content as I tend to be
in both darkness and in light.

黄昏に
するりと我を
覆う影
ひかり巡れず
間合い甘受す

Along the dark lane
a girl passed in shadow
and I heard her sneeze.
"Bless you", I said from my side,
and from hers a small giggle.

One foot in the dark,
the other in full bright light,
this path that I walk.
I see no clear turns ahead,
but wait to see which claims me.

明暗を
一足ごとに
歩む道
無明の先に
我を待つもの

One night, in the rain,
I stood outside my own house
hidden in shadow,
savoring the warm light and
music coming from inside.

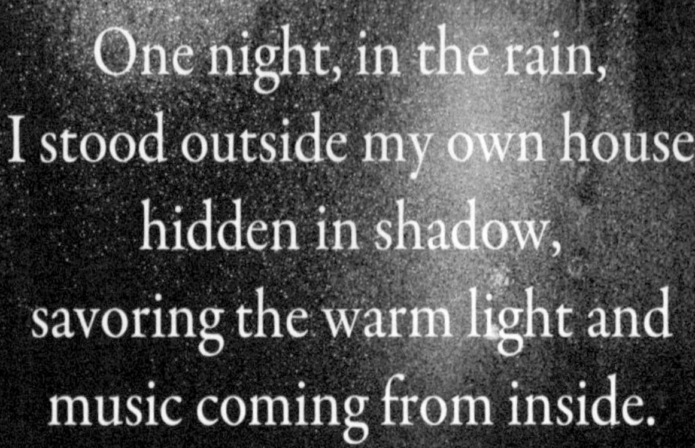

雨夜影
庭に漏れ来る
うるおしき
調べと光に
闇と佇む

Three o'clock woke me,
the street empty and quiet,
leading to shadows.
That long walk to the darkness
tempted me but no, not yet.

The windows go dim,
one by one the rooms go dark,
movement seems to cease.
There's still life in there somewhere,
but it gets harder to find.

Deep night balcony,
savoring a plum yogurt,
listening to crickets,
gazing into the darkness,
no need to go back to bed.

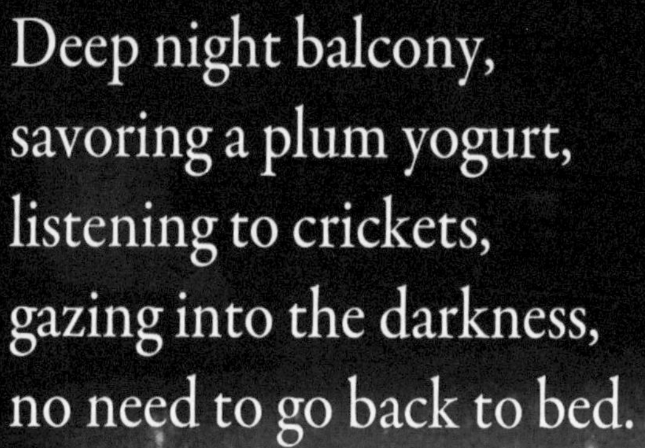

更深や
闇に奏づる
虫の音に
プラムヨーグルト飲み
現つ夜を過ぐ

Morning light fades fast
and edges become muted
as day becomes dusk.
It's when one feels most alone,
as shadows lengthen into night.

Tonight's crescent moon
suddenly hidden from me
by dark passing clouds.
I recall happier places
now obscured by passing years.

三日月や
雲の切れ間に
かき消えぬ
ふと愛おしき
あの時と場所

Shadows on shadows
overlapping as we go,
passing unnoticed,
here for a moment then gone,
mere reflections, illusions.

All sorts of shadows
flutter and glide on the pavement,
a kind of harmony.
Who cares what they're shadows of,
for each shares in my darkness.

For just an instant,
we leave behind our shadows
and they too vanish.
We have been and that's enough,
it's our own sweet, sad beauty.

We are but shadows
moving lightly, fleetingly
over the surface.
Noticed by some, barely seen,
they look again and we're gone.

陰おぼろ
地を薄々と
まろびけん
現われ消えしぞ
我れ儚きや

Drinking my coffee
contemplating a moody sky,
the light quickly fades.
I wait and watch for the sun,
that shines just beyond the clouds.

去来せる
遠間近間の
我が闇に
一条来たらむ
光煌々（こうこう）

We are mesmerized
by the passing of shadows.
light yielding to dark.
And we too are part shadow,
yet from us, sometimes, comes light.

I've lived in shadows,
exiled to them for so long,
that I'm one myself.
Though I love all that is light,
I can't belong to it again.

Warming my cold hands
over my cup, I gaze through
my foggy windows
and feel, not unpleasantly,
all the autumns of my life.

My eyes cast downward,
a shadow darting here, there —
a small butterfly.
Glancing up I spotted it,
touching my hat and then gone.

吾が愛でる
瞬間（またたき）の音（ね）の
根に秘（ひ）そぐ
くぐもりの声
光裂く闇

These things I cherish:
the moment between glances;
stillness beneath sound;
the voice of the unuttered;
the darkness behind the light.

Each late afternoon
is an autumn in itself —
golden light, hushed tones.
Days and loves and lives all end
in very much the same way.

Out in the evening
for the first time in too long,
a world I'd forgotten.
I was a tourist of the night,
stopped in my tracks by the moon.

I long for the sound
of no sound, of deep silence,
that I might listen
to the voice of the universe,
in the stillness between all things.

About Michael Boiano

An Italian-American from New York who currently lives in Bangkok, Thailand, Michael Boiano worked as a clinical psychotherapist at several American universities before moving to Asia to pursue a second career in teaching. In Japan, he lived in Sendai and travelled extensively in Japan and felt an affinity with Japanese culture, aesthetics, and Tanka poetry. James Kirkup, who was a well known poet and teacher in Japan encouraged Michael's poetry and wrote an introduction to Michael's first poetry book (Gajin Diary, 2018). Michael became a regular contributor to "The Tanka Journal" in Tokyo and has won awards for his poetry. Currently, he teaches — he introduces Tanka poetry to his students — and, like many of the Japanese poets he most admired, he lives a life of simplicity and contemplation.

Michael writes about longing, solitude, nature and struggle with humor, insight, sensitivity and a "wabi-sabi" sensibility. His poems are written in traditional 5-7-5-7-7 form with a melodic rhythm rich with deeper meanings and fleeting impressions inspired by his love of nature and by his daily struggles to survive in Thailand. Each of his poems is a miniature that creates a little universe of its own, a place to stay for a while to ponder in silence. His work will resonate with readers of all ages, no matter if they are from Japan or elsewhere.

Some of Michael's poems are published on his tumblr blog "Aki no Niwa" (see www.aki-no-niwa.tumblr.com). He can be reached at tankapoetbkk@gmail.com. His Line ID is "poetandteacher".

Author (tanka): Michael Boiano (tankapoetbkk@gmail.com)
Japanese translations: Daijiro
Background photos and design: Jumy-M
Front cover image: Jana Sojka (http://janasojka.com)
Book design and editing: Job Honig (blackturtlepress@gmail.com)

Publisher: Black Turtle Press, Taiwan
Edition: 1st, August 2020
ISBN: 978-986-99284-0-3

black turtle press

taoyuan (daxi), taiwan